ANGELS
Billy Graham

ANGELS

Copyright © 1996 by Garborg's Heart 'n Home, Inc.

Excerpts used by permission of Word Publishing, Dallas, TX

Published by Garborg's Heart 'n Home, Inc.
P. O. Box 20132, Bloomington, MN 55420

Design by Franke Design Co.

All rights reserved. No part of this book may be reproduced in any form
without permission in writing from the publisher.

All Scripture quotations, unless otherwise noted, are taken from The Holy Bible,
King James Version.

Scripture quotations marked NIV are taken from the HOLY BIBLE, NEW INTERNATIONAL
VERSION® NIV®. Copyright © 1973, 1978, 1984 by International Bible Society.
All rights reserved.

Scripture quotations marked TLB are taken from the The Living Bible © 1971. Used by permission
of Tyndale House Publishers, Inc., Wheaton, IL 60189. All rights reserved.

SPCN 5-5044-0300-6

Yes, angels are real. They are not the product of our imagination, but were made by God himself. Think of it! Whether we see them or not, God has created a vast host of angels to help accomplish His work in this world.

JANUARY 1

Behold, I am coming soon! Blessed is he who keeps the words of the prophecy in this book.

REVELATION 22:7 NIV

DECEMBER 31

The spirit world and its activities are big news today. And the idea of the supernatural is not only seriously regarded, but is accepted as a fact. Many of the most recent books on the subject border on the sensational, or are purely speculative, or have been dreamed up in somebody's imagination.

JANUARY 2

Do you have that hope of eternity in your heart right now? Do you know—beyond doubt—that someday you will join the angels in heaven in singing praises to God?... This can happen, if you will give your life to Christ and trust Him as your personal Lord and Savior.... Right now by a simple prayer of faith you can know that someday you will join with the angels and with millions of believers from across the ages in singing praises to God in heaven. Take that step of faith today.

DECEMBER 30

Even when people in our modern age have had their
attention drawn to the subject of angels from time
to time, those ideas have often been fanciful or
unbiblical.... But the Bible stresses their reality
and underlines their constant—if unseen—
ministry on behalf of God's people.

JANUARY 3

The keynote of evangelism is couched in the heavenly proclamation I have mentioned, "Unto you is born this day...a Saviour which is Christ the Lord." And the task of world evangelization will be completed by men and women whom the Holy Spirit uses.

DECEMBER 29

$\mathcal{J}$ust a few years ago such ideas would have been scorned by most educated people. Science was king, and science was tuned in to believe only what could be seen or measured. The idea of supernatural beings was thought to be nonsense, the ravings of the lunatic fringe. All this has changed.

JANUARY 4

"A multitude of the heavenly host" began to chant or sing, "Glory to God in the highest, and on earth peace, good will toward men." Where could there be sweeter music? What hymn writer could match those words?

DECEMBER 28

In a materialistic world which nevertheless is riddled with evil and suffering, we need to discover afresh the Bible's teaching about angels.

Preserve sound judgment and discernment, do not let them out of your sight.

PROVERBS 3:21 NIV

JANUARY 5

The good tidings were that the Savior had come....
The angel message was that God had come,
redemption was possible, the Lord had
visited His people with salvation.

DECEMBER 27

Speculation about the nature of angels has been around since long before Queen Victoria's time, and it continues down to the present time. Yet through revelation in the Bible God has told us a great deal about them.

JANUARY 6

What did the angel say? First, he brought good tidings, not bad ones. The shepherds already knew the bad news—the human race had sinned and was lost. But the angel had come to tell them that God was doing something about their lostness. And he pointed out that...
the good tidings were for all people.

DECEMBER 26

I am convinced that these heavenly beings exist and that they provide unseen aid on our behalf.... I believe in angels because the Bible says there are angels; and I believe the Bible to be the true Word of God.

JANUARY 7

Throughout all time, this divine declaration of Gabriel shall be the Magna Charta of the incarnation and the foundation stone of the world to come: God became flesh to redeem us.

You will be with child and give birth to a son, and you are to give him the name Jesus.... The holy one to be born will be called the Son of God."

LUKE 1:31,35 NIV

DECEMBER 25

See that you do not look down on one of these little ones. For I tell you that their angels in heaven always see the face of my Father in heaven.

MATTHEW 18:10 NIV

JANUARY 8

When the angel had quieted the fears of the shepherds, he brought this message, one forever to be connected with the evangel:

Behold I bring you good tidings of great joy, which shall be to all people. For unto you is born this day in the city of David a Saviour, which is Christ the Lord.

LUKE 2:10,11

DECEMBER 24

In the midst of a world which seems destined to live in a perpetual state of crisis, the subject of angels will be of great comfort and inspiration to believers in God— and a challenge for unbelievers to believe.

JANUARY 9

What was the message of the angel to the shepherds? First, he told them not to be afraid. Over and over again the presence of angels was frightening to those to whom they came. But unless they came in judgment, the angels spoke a word of reassurance. They calmed the people to whom they came.

DECEMBER 23

As an evangelist, I have often felt too far spent to minister from the pulpit to men and women who have filled stadiums to hear a message from the Lord.... On many occasions, God has become especially real, and has sent His unseen angelic visitors to touch my body to let me be His messenger for heaven, speaking as a dying man to dying men.

JANUARY 10

Does it not seem mysterious that God brought the first message of the birth of Jesus to ordinary people rather than to princes and kings? In this instance, God spoke through His holy angel to the shepherds.... But Mary in her song, the Magnificat, tells us the true story: "He hath put down the mighty from their seats, and exalted them of low degree" (Luke 1:52). What a word for our generation!

DECEMBER 22

It is my prayer that you will discover the reality of God's love and care for you as evidenced in the ministry of His angels on your behalf.

JANUARY 11

How beautifully the prophecies of the Old Testament are linked together with the fulfillment in the New Testament. How gracious God was to use His angels as agents to make it plain to all they visited in all ages that their business was to witness to the evangel.

DECEMBER 21

In *A Slow and Certain Light*, Elizabeth Elliot told about her father's experiences with angelic helpers:

My father, when he was a small boy, was climbing on an upper story of a house that was being built. He walked to the end of a board that was not nailed at the other end, and it slowly began to tip. He knew that he was doomed, but inexplicably the board began to tip the other way, as though a hand had pushed it down again. He always wondered if it was an angel's hand.

JANUARY 12

In the midst of the wonder of the incarnation we should not overlook the fact that the angel was here bearing witness to the "evangel," the gospel. Jesus was not coming simply as God. He was coming as Redeemer and Savior to make men right with His Father and to assure them of the gift of everlasting life.

DECEMBER 20

Sir Edward Coley Burne-Jones wrote "the more materialistic science becomes, the more angels shall I paint: their wings are my protest in favor of the immortality of the soul."

JANUARY 13

According to the witness of the angel, sins can be forgiven. There is someone who can forgive sins. This is Jesus the Christ. The Savior has a people about whom He is concerned and guarantees that their sins will be forgiven.

DECEMBER 19

Angels have a much more important place in the Bible than the devil and his demons. Therefore, I undertook a biblical study on the subject of angels. Not only has it been one of the most fascinating studies of my life, but I believe the subject is more relevant today than perhaps at any time in history.

JANUARY 14

The Scripture says that...an angel appeared to [Joseph] in a dream and told him the true story of the incarnation and the role of Mary. Responding, Joseph believed the angel. But the announcement contained more than the simple fact that Mary was innocent of any transgression and that Joseph was the chosen vessel of God in affording her protection in this extraordinary event.

DECEMBER 18

Witness the unprecedented and unrepeated pageantry at Mount Sinai. When God moves toward man, it is an event of the first magnitude and can include the visitation of angelic hosts. In the billowing clouds that covered Sinai an angelic trumpeter announced the presence of God. The whole mountain seemed to pulsate with life.

The sight was so terrifying that Moses said,
"I am trembling with fear."
HEBREWS 12:21 NIV

JANUARY 15

The angel also told Joseph something that was to witness to the gospel. Though the angel could not preach to Joseph, he struck at the root of the matter when he proclaimed, "He shall save his people from their sins" (Matthew 1:21). Here was the gospel in all of its beauty, simplicity, and purity.

DECEMBER 17

*A*ngels are created spirit beings who can become
visible when necessary. They can appear and disappear.
They think, feel, will, and display emotions.

JANUARY 16

[Mary] cries out that God's "mercy is on them that fear him from generation to generation." What is this but the glorious evangel, [which means the] gospel, that God was in Christ reconciling the world to himself? And this was the message Gabriel brought to Mary.

DECEMBER 16

It would take an entire book to spell out in detail how the life of Jesus was intertwined with the attending ministry of angels. Before He was here, they followed His orders. And since He ascended into heaven, they have worshiped Him before the throne of God as the Lamb slain for our salvation.

JANUARY 17

The very baby who was encased in [Mary's] womb would one day offer himself as a propitiation for her and for all men. And that baby in her womb was God Almighty who had humbled himself in order to dwell among us in the flesh.

DECEMBER 15

The angel of the Lord encamps around those who fear him, and he delivers them.

PSALM 34:7 NIV

JANUARY 18

"My spirit hath rejoiced in God my Saviour" (Luke 1:47). Here was the news that Mary herself needed a Savior, and had found Him.

DECEMBER 14

God has commissioned these angels to aid His children in their struggles…. The Bible does not give as much information about them as we might like, but what it does say should be a source of comfort and strength for us in every circumstance.

JANUARY 19

The angel told Mary that Jesus would be the Son of the Highest, that He would inherit the throne of His father David, would reign over the house of Jacob forever, and would be an everlasting kingdom. This was something far different from anything promised anyone else in Scripture.... Only Jesus' name is connected with these promises.

DECEMBER 13

𝒜ngels guide, comfort, and provide for
the people of God in the midst of suffering
and persecution.

JANUARY 20

In his most important appearance, Gabriel informs the Virgin Mary about Jesus, the incarnate God! What a message to deliver to the world through a teenage girl! What a wonderfully holy girl she must have been, to be visited by the mighty Gabriel.

God sent the angel Gabriel to Nazareth, a town in Galilee to a virgin.... And said, "Greetings, you who are highly favored! The Lord is with you."

LUKE 1:26,28 NIV

DECEMBER 12

What I have to say...will not be an accumulation of my ideas about the spirit world, nor even a reflection of my own spiritual experiences in the spirit realm. I propose to put forward, at least in part, what I understand the Bible to say about angels.

JANUARY 21

The announcement to Mary that she was to be the mother of Jesus was made by no ordinary angel. It was Gabriel, one of three angels whose names have been given us in Scripture, who made the announcement.

DECEMBER 11

A Persian colporteur was accosted by a man who asked him if he had a right to sell Bibles. "Why yes," he answered, "we are allowed to sell these books anywhere in the country!" The man looked puzzled and asked, "How is it, then, that you are always surrounded by soldiers? I planned three times to attack you and each time, seeing the soldiers, I left you alone. Now I no longer want to harm you." Were these soldiers heavenly beings?

JANUARY 22

The appearance of God the Son in physical form (a theophany) in the Old Testament is no longer necessary. Consider the presence of angels in the New Testament subsequent to the thrilling account of the birth of God the Son in the flesh through His incarnation at Bethlehem. The angels then were to minister the message of God and to establish the message of the gospel of Christ, but never to supplant it or to detract from it.

DECEMBER 10

God is just: He will...give relief to you who are troubled, and to us as well. This will happen when the Lord Jesus is revealed from heaven in blazing fire with his powerful angels. He will punish those who do not know God.

2 THESSALONIANS 1:6-8 NIV

JANUARY 23

In most instances, angels, when appearing visibly, are so glorious and impressively beautiful as to stun and amaze men who witness their presence.

There were shepherds living out in the fields nearby....
An angel of the Lord appeared to them, and the glory
of the Lord shone around them, and they were terrified.

LUKE 2:8,9 NIV

DECEMBER 9

This will not be an exhaustive study on the subject of angels. I hope, however, that it will arouse your curiosity sufficiently for you to dig out from the Bible all that you can find on this subject.

JANUARY 24

The charge to live righteously in this present world
sobers us when we realize that the walk and warfare
of Christians is the primary concern of heaven
and its angelic hosts.

DECEMBER 8

$\mathcal{T}$he Scriptures do not support the common belief that all angels have wings. The traditional concept of angels with wings is drawn from their ability to move instantaneously and with unlimited speed from place to place, and wings were thought to permit such limitless movement.

JANUARY 25

$\mathcal{G}$od is watching, and His angels are interested spectators too. The Amplified Bible expresses 1 Corinthians 4:9 this way: "God has made an exhibit of us...a show in the world's amphitheater—with both men and angels (as spectators)." We know they are watching, but in the heat of the battle, I have thought how wonderful it would be if we could hear them cheering.

DECEMBER 7

If we, the sons of God, would only realize how close His ministering angels are, what calm assurance we could have in facing the cataclysms of life.

JANUARY 26

[As the angels watch us], what are they thinking as we live in the world's arena? Do they observe us as we stand fast in the faith and walk in righteousness? Or may they be wondering at our lack of commitment?... Our certainty that angels right now witness how we are walking through life should mightily influence the decisions we make.

DECEMBER 6

*S*piritual forces and resources are available to all Christians. Because our resources are unlimited, Christians will be winners.

JANUARY 27

Angel hosts have witnessed the formation of the church of Christ Jesus, and have watched the walk of each believer as the Lord worked His grace, love, and power into each life. The angels are observing firsthand the building of the body of the true church in all places of His dominion this very hour.

DECEMBER 5

Some biblical scholars believe that angels can be numbered potentially in the millions since Hebrews 12:22 speaks of "an innumerable [myriads—a great but indefinite number] company of angels."

You have come to Mount Zion and to the city of the living God, the heavenly Jerusalem, to an innumerable company of angels.

HEBREWS 12:22 NKJV

JANUARY 28

Be strong! Be courageous! Don't be afraid, for the Lord will go before you and will be with you. He will neither fail you nor forsake you.

DEUTERONOMY 31:6 TLB

DECEMBER 4

*M*atthew Henry says…"Angels are 'the chariots of God,' His chariots of war, which He makes use of against His enemies, His chariots of conveyance, which He sends for His friends, as He did for Elijah…His chariots of state, in the midst of which He shows His glory and power. They are vastly numerous: 'Twenty thousands,' even thousands multiplied."

JANUARY 29

We face many perplexing questions today, such as: Why does God permit evil?... Yet God's timing is precise! Angel hosts who witness everything that transpires in our world are not free to bear up the righteous and deliver the oppressed until God gives the signal. One day He will.

DECEMBER 3

Those who take the Bible at full value cannot discount the subject of angels as speculation or hollow conjecture. After all, the Scriptures mention their existence almost three hundred times.

JANUARY 30

Psalm 34:7 underscores the teaching that angels protect and deliver us, "The angel of the Lord encampeth round about those who fear him, and delivereth them."

DECEMBER 2

$\mathcal{T}$he apostle Paul has said in Colossians 2:15 (NKJV), "Having disarmed principalities and powers, he made a show of them openly, triumphing over them."

JANUARY 31

God is not called "Father" by the holy angels because, not having sinned, they need not be redeemed.... The term is normally reserved in Scripture for lost men who have been redeemed. So in a real sense, even ordinary men cannot call God "Father," except as their Creator God—until they are born again.

DECEMBER 1

$\mathcal{V}$ictory over the flesh, the world, and the devil is ours now! The angels are here to help, and they are prepared for any emergency.

FEBRUARY 1

If you are a believer, expect powerful angels to accompany you in your life experiences. And let those events dramatically illustrate the friendly presence of "the holy ones," as Daniel calls them.

NOVEMBER 30

As you read this book, I pray that God will open
your eyes to the resources He has provided for
all who turn to Him for strength.

FEBRUARY 2

I believe that death can be beautiful. I have come to look forward to it, to anticipate it with joy and expectation. I have stood at the side of many people who died with expressions of triumph on their faces. No wonder the Bible says, "Precious in the sight of the Lord is the death of his saints" (Psalm 116:16).

NOVEMBER 29

We may not always be aware of the presence of angels. We can't always predict how they will appear. But angels have been said to be our neighbors. Often they may be our companions without our being aware of their presence.

FEBRUARY 3

When the apostle Paul spoke of his own approaching death, he said, "We are confident, I say, and willing rather to be absent from the body, and to be present with the Lord" (2 Corinthians 5:8). When that glorious physical and spiritual separation takes place, the angels will be there to escort us into the presence of our Savior with abounding joy, and it will mean "life everlasting."

NOVEMBER 28

The Son is the radiance of God's glory and the exact representation of his being, sustaining all things by his powerful word.... When God brings his firstborn into the world, he says, "Let all God's angels worship him."

HEBREWS 1:3,6 NIV

FEBRUARY 4

We must be aware that angels keep in close and vital
contact with all that is happening on the earth. Their
knowledge of earthly matters exceeds that of men.
We must attest to their invisible presence
and unceasing labors.

NOVEMBER 27

The apostle Paul understood and spoke of the war of rebellion in the heavens when he referred to the former Lucifer, now Satan, as "the prince of the power of the air, the spirit that now worketh in the children of disobedience" (Ephesians 2:2).

FEBRUARY 5

We can look for that future day when angels will have finished their earthly ministry. Then they will gather with all the redeemed before the throne of God in heaven.... In that day the angels who veiled their faces and stood mute when Jesus hung on the cross will then ascribe glory to the Lamb whose work is finished and whose kingdom has come.

NOVEMBER 26

Abraham, Lot, Jacob, and others had no difficulty recognizing angels when God allowed them to manifest themselves in physical form. Note, for example, Jacob's instant recognition of angels in Genesis 32:1,2: "And Jacob went on his way, and the angels of God met him. And when Jacob saw them, he said, This is God's host."

FEBRUARY 6

The glorious Holy Spirit can be everywhere at the same time, but no angel can be in more than one place at any given moment.

NOVEMBER 25

The Bible tells us that God has made man "a little lower than the angels." Yet it also says angels are "ministering spirits, sent forth to minister for them who shall be heirs of salvation" (Hebrews 2:5-7; 1:13-14).

FEBRUARY 7

Don't let anyone deceive you in any way.... The lawless one will be revealed, whom the Lord Jesus will overthrow with the breath of his mouth and destroy by the splendor of his coming. The coming of the lawless one will be in accordance with the work of Satan displayed in all kinds of counterfeit miracles, signs and wonders.

2 THESSALONIANS 2:3,8,9 NIV

NOVEMBER 24

Christians are joint heirs with Jesus Christ through redemption (Romans 8:17), which is made theirs by faith in Him based on His death at Calvary. Angels who are not joint heirs must stand aside when the believers are introduced to their boundless, eternal riches.

FEBRUARY 8

Angels...are not omnipresent...so they can be in only one place at a given time. Yet as God's messengers they are busy around the world carrying out God's orders. Is it not, therefore, obvious that when they are engaged in their ministry here they cannot stand before God's throne? But when angels do stand before the throne of God, indeed they worship and adore their Creator.

NOVEMBER 23

Although some interpreters have said that the phrase "sons of God" in Genesis 6:2 refers to angels, the Bible frequently makes it clear that angels are nonmaterial; Hebrews 1:14 calls them ministering "spirits."

Are they not all ministering spirits sent to serve those who will inherit salvation.

HEBREWS 1:14 NIV

FEBRUARY 9

*E*ve foolishly parleyed with the tempter. In her own mind she began to doubt the truth and the wisdom of God. How easily Satan covers with a light color ideas that are dark. His intrigue comes to us colored in the light of our own desires.

NOVEMBER 22

$\mathcal{H}$e has given angels higher knowledge,
power, and mobility than we.

FEBRUARY 10

𝒯en thousand angels came down on Mount Sinai to confirm the holy presence of God as He gave the Law to Moses (Deuteronomy 33:2). An earthquake shook the mountain. Moses was held in speech-bound wonder at this mighty cataclysm attended by the visitation of heavenly beings.

*The Lord came to us at Mount Sinai…
surrounded by ten thousands of holy angels,
and with flaming fire at his right hand.*

DEUTERONOMY 33:2 TLB

NOVEMBER 21

Have you ever seen or met one of these superior beings called angels? Probably not, for both the Bible and human experience tell us visible appearances by angels are very rare—but that in no way makes angels any less real or powerful.

FEBRUARY 11

*W*herever and whenever we see the gospel working in its power to transform, there is a possibility that in some ways angels may be involved.

NOVEMBER 20

Angels are God's messengers whose chief business is to carry out His orders in the world. He has given them an ambassadorial charge.

FEBRUARY 12

Although angels are glorious beings, the Scriptures make it clear that they differ from regenerated men in significant ways. How can the angels who have never sinned fully understand what it means to be delivered from sin?

NOVEMBER 19

God has designated and empowered angels as holy deputies to perform works of righteousness. In this way they assist Him as their creator while He sovereignly controls the universe.

FEBRUARY 13

We will find no final solution to the world's great problems until this spiritual warfare [between God's forces of good and Satan's forces of evil] has been settled. And it will be settled in the last war of history—Armageddon. Then Christ and His angelic armies will be the victor!

NOVEMBER 18

*G*od has given angels the capacity to bring His holy enterprises to a successful conclusion.

FEBRUARY 14

The Bible speaks about a city whose builder and maker is God, where those who have been redeemed will be superior to angels. It speaks of "a pure river of water of life, clear as crystal proceeding out of the throne of God and of the Lamb" (Revelation 22:1).

NOVEMBER 17

𝒟on't believe everything you hear (and read!) about angels! Some would have us believe that they are only spiritual will-o'-the wisps. Some view them as only celestial beings with beautiful wings and bowed heads. Others would have us think of them as effeminate weirdos.

FEBRUARY 15

*M*any years ago I was visiting the dining room of the United States Senate. As I was speaking to various people, one of the senators called me to his table. He said, "Billy, we're having a discussion about pessimism and optimism. Are you a pessimist or an optimist?" I smiled and said, "I'm an optimist." He asked, "Why?" I said, "I've read the last page of the Bible."

NOVEMBER 16

The Bible states that angels, like men, were created by God. At one time no angels existed; indeed there was nothing but the Triune God: Father, Son, and Holy Spirit. Paul, in Colossians 1:16, says, "For by him were all things created, that are in heaven, and that are in earth, visible and invisible."

FEBRUARY 16

I saw four angels standing at the four corners of the earth, holding back the four winds of the earth to prevent any wind from blowing on the land or on the sea or on any tree. Then I saw another angel coming up from the east, having the seal of the living God. He called out in a loud voice to the four angels who had been given power to harm the land and the sea: "Do not harm the land or the sea or the trees until we put a seal on the foreheads of the servants of our God."

REVELATION 7:1-3 NIV

NOVEMBER 15

Angels indeed are among the invisible things
made by God, for "all things were created
by Him, and for Him."

FEBRUARY 17

$\mathcal{T}$he Book of Revelation, from chapter 4 to 19, gives us a picture of judgments to befall the earth such as the world has never known. Angels will be involved in all of these judgments. But after these terrifying events, Christ will come with His holy angels to set up His kingdom.

NOVEMBER 14

Even angels would cease to exist if Jesus, who is Almighty God, did not sustain them by His power.

He is before all things, and in him all things consist.

COLOSSIANS 1:17 NIV

FEBRUARY 18

"The marriage supper of the Lamb." This is the great event when Jesus Christ is crowned King of kings and Lord of lords. Both believers of all ages and all the angelic hosts will join in bowing their knees and confessing that He is Lord.

NOVEMBER 13

It seems that angels have the ability to change their appearance and shuttle in a flash from the capital glory of heaven to earth and back again.

FEBRUARY 19

𝒥esus taught that "Whosoever shall confess me before men, him shall the Son of man also confess before the angels of God" (Luke 12:8).

NOVEMBER 12

*J*esus said…"I tell you the truth, you shall see heaven open, and the angels of God ascending and descending on the Son of Man."

JOHN 1:50,51 NIV

FEBRUARY 20

We are not left in doubt about who will ultimately triumph. Time after time Jesus has assured us that He and the angels would be victorious. "When the Son of man shall come in his glory, and all the holy angels with him, then shall he sit upon the throne of his glory."

NOVEMBER 11

$\mathcal{A}$t the same time, both angels and the Holy Spirit
are at work in our world to accomplish God's perfect will.
Frankly, we may not always know the agent or means
God is using—the Holy Spirit or the angels—
when we discern God's hand at work.

FEBRUARY 21

*M*any times throughout biblical history, and possibly
even today, angels and demons engage in warfare.
Many of the events of our times may very
well be involved in this unseen struggle.

NOVEMBER 10

$\mathcal{A}$ngels belong to a uniquely different dimension of creation that we, limited to the natural order, can scarcely comprehend. In this angelic domain the limitations are different from those God has imposed on our natural order.

FEBRUARY 22

While angels have tremendous authority, it is limited to doing only the will of God. They never deviate from God's plan. Throughout the ages they have glorified only Him, never themselves.

NOVEMBER 9

*O*f one thing we can be sure: angels never draw attention to themselves but ascribe glory to God and press His message upon the hearers as a delivering and sustaining word of the highest order.

FEBRUARY 23

We find the answer to the future in Holy Scripture. It is summed up in the person of Jesus Christ. God has centered all our hopes and dreams on Him. He is the Commander in Chief of these angelic armies that will accompany Him on His return.

NOVEMBER 8

To His "faithful" of past ages, God the Father revealed His presence through angels; through the angel of the Lord, God the Son, Jesus Christ, He revealed himself and redeemed us by the Son's crucifixion, death, and resurrection. Here is mystery too deep for any of us to fathom fully.

JULY 1

God has given us the fullest revelation—Jesus Christ in the flesh—so He no longer needs to manifest himself in the form of "the angel of the Lord" in this age of grace. Consequently, the angels who appear in the New Testament or even today are always "created spirits" and not God in that special angel form.

JULY 2

God still sends angels to guard His children in their hour of danger.

JULY 3

When the angel Lucifer rebelled against God and His works, some have estimated that as many as one-third of the angelic hosts of the universe may have joined him in his rebellion. Thus, the war that started in heaven continues on earth and will see its climax at Armageddon with Christ and His angelic army victorious.

JUNE 30

Leslie Miller in his excellent little book, *All About Angels*, points out that Scripture sometimes refers to angels as stars. This explains why prior to his fall Satan was called "the star of the morning." And to this description John adds a qualifying detail, "His tail swept a third of the stars out of the sky and flung them to the earth" (Revelation 12:4, NIV).

JULY 4

It may well be that some of these instances [when angels appeared] involved angelic forms taken by Jesus Christ, the second person of the Trinity. We can only speculate. In that event, it makes alive the thrilling testimony of Paul who declared that "Jesus Christ [is] the same yesterday, and today, and forever" (Hebrews 13:8).

JUNE 29

What a glorious honor it will be for angels to know us by name because of our faithful witness to others. Angels will share our rejoicing over those who repent (Luke 15:10), even though they cannot preach the gospel themselves.

JULY 5

The One whom God chose and anointed before time began will return to earth with His mighty, holy angels. At the end of the age He will throw the devil and his demons into the lake of fire. Thus, for the true believer the conflict now raging will end as God intends. Righteousness will prevail.

JUNE 28

Consider Philip the deacon, whom God was using as a minister of revival in Samaria. An angel appeared with instructions for him to go to the desert (Acts 8:26), and by God's appointment he met the Ethiopian to whom he became the voice for God in preaching the word of truth.

JULY 6

$\mathcal{O}$ne day the angels came to present themselves
before the Lord, and Satan also came with them.
The Lord said to Satan, "Where have you come from?"
Satan answered the Lord, "From roaming through
the earth and going back and forth in it."

JOB 1:6,7 NIV

JUNE 27

𝒜ngels visited John too. As he looked out upon the lonely seas from the Isle of Patmos and wondered why he was isolated from all but heaven, the angel of the apocalypse came to announce the message that formed the Book of Revelation with its prophecies of the end time (Revelation 1:1-3).

JULY 7

The conflict of the ages will be resolved only when Jesus Christ returns to the earth. This is why the world is crying for "a leader." The Anti-Christ, who will be Satan's "front," will arrive on the scene for a brief time and seemingly be "The Answer." But after only a few months the world will be thrown back into chaos and conflict. He will prove to be "The Lie."

JUNE 26

Few people realize the profound part angelic forces play in human events. It is Daniel who most dramatically reveals the constant and bitter conflict between the holy angels faithful to God and the angels of darkness allied with Satan.

A hand touched me and set me trembling on my hands and knees. He continued, "Do not be afraid, Daniel. Since the first day that you set your mind to gain understanding and to humble yourself before your God, your words were heard, and I have come in response to them."

DANIEL 10:10,11 NIV

JULY 8

Many experiences of God's people suggest that angels have been ministering to them. Others may not have known they were being helped, yet the visitation was real. The Bible tells us that God has ordered angels to minister to His people—those who have been redeemed by the power of Christ's blood.

JUNE 25

God's restoring servants, His heavenly messengers, have encouraged, sustained, and lifted the spirits of many flagging saints; and they have changed many hopeless circumstances into bright prospects.

JULY 9

We know little of the angels' constant ministry.
The Bible assures us, however, that one day our eyes
will be unscaled to see and know the full extent
of the attention angels have given us.

When perfection comes, the imperfect disappears....
Now I know in part; then I shall know fully,
even as I am fully known.

1 CORINTHIANS 13:10,12 NIV

JUNE 24

They will see the Son of Man coming on the clouds of the sky, with power and great glory.... No one knows about that day or hour, not even the angels in heaven, nor the Son, but only the Father.

MATTHEW 24:30,36 NIV

JULY 10

𝒫rior to his rebellion, Lucifer, an angel of light, is described in scintillating terms in Ezekiel 28:12-17 (NASB): "You had the seal of perfection, full of wisdom and perfect in beauty.... You were blameless in your ways from the day you were created, until unrighteousness was found in you.... Your heart was lifted up because of your beauty; you corrupted your wisdom by reason of your splendor."

JUNE 23

The enemies of Christ who attack us incessantly would often be thwarted if we could grasp God's assurance that His mighty angels are always nearby, ready to help. Tragically, most Christians have failed to accept this fact so frequently expressed in the Bible.

JULY 11

I pray that God will...show you your constant need of Him, and how He has sent His Son, Jesus Christ, into the world to deliver you from both the guilt and power of sin.

JUNE 22

I have noticed that in my travels the closer I get to the frontiers of the Christian faith the more faith in angels I find among believers. Hundreds of stories document extraordinary divine intervention every year: God is using His angels as ministering spirits.

JULY 12

Only when we turn to Christ in faith and trust, confessing our sins to Him and seeking His forgiveness, can we be assured of our salvation. Satan will do all in his power to make us trust ourselves instead of Christ. But only Christ can save us—and He will, if we will commit our lives to Him and trust His work on the cross for our salvation.

JUNE 21

𝒢od's angels often protect His servants from potential enemies.... The angels minister to God's servants in time of hardship and danger.... Some believe strongly that each Christian may have his own guardian angel assigned to watch over him or her. This guardianship possibly begins in infancy, for Jesus said, "Take heed that ye despise not one of these little ones; for I say unto you, that in heaven their angels do always behold the face of my Father" (Matthew 18:10).

JULY 13

Death for the Christian cuts the cord that holds us captive in this present evil world so that angels may transport believers to their heavenly inheritance. Death is the fiery chariot, the gentle voice of the King, the invitation to nonstop passage into the banquet house of the world of glory.

JUNE 20

The most important characteristic of angels is not that they have power to exercise control over our lives, or that they are beautiful, but that they work on our behalf.

JULY 14

When we know God personally through faith in His Son, Jesus Christ, we can have confidence that the angels of God will watch over us and assist us because we belong to Him.

JUNE 19

Angels are motivated by an inexhaustible love for God and are jealous to see that the will of God in Jesus Christ is fulfilled in us.

JULY 15

*O*ur ability to sense reality is limited....
So why should we think it strange if men fail
to perceive the evidences of angelic presence?

JUNE 18

David says of angels, "He who dwelleth in the secret place of the Most High shall abide under the shadow of the Almighty.... For he shall give his angels charge over thee, to keep thee in all thy ways. They shall bear thee up...lest thou dash thy foot against a stone" (Psalm 91:1,11,12).

JULY 16

*M*an must do his best in meting out justice, but his best is not complete justice. To angels will be delegated the ministry of separating the good from the bad [when Christ returns], discerning even attitudes.

JUNE 17

Are you ready to face life? Are you ready to face death? No one is truly ready to die who has not learned to live for the glory of God. You can put your confidence in Jesus because He died for you, and in that last moment—the greatest crisis of all—He will have His angels gather you in their arms to carry you gloriously, wonderfully into heaven.

JULY 17

Gabriel is primarily God's messenger of mercy and promise. He appears four times in the Bible, always bearing good news.... The announcement of Gabriel in unfolding the plans, purposes, and verdicts of God is of monumental importance.

The angel answered, "I am Gabriel. I stand in the presence of God, and I have been sent to speak to you and to tell you this good news."

LUKE 1:19 NIV

JUNE 16

𝒜ngels are interested spectators and mark all we do, "for we are made a spectacle unto the world, and to angels, and to men" (1 Corinthians 4:9). God assigns angelic powers to watch over us.

JULY 18

*I*n his *Institutes*, John Calvin said, "The angels are the dispensers and administrators of the Divine beneficence toward us; they regard our safety, undertake our defense, direct our ways, and exercise a constant solicitude that no evil befall us."

JUNE 15

$\mathcal{H}$ow would you live if you knew that you were being watched all the time, not only by your parents, wife, husband, or children, but by the heavenly host? The Bible teaches...that angels are watching us.

JULY 19

$\mathcal{L}$ucifer was the most brilliant and most beautiful of all created beings in heaven. He was probably the ruling prince of the universe under God, against whom he rebelled. The result was insurrection and war in heaven! He began a war that has been raging in heaven from the moment he sinned and was brought to earth shortly after the dawn of human history.

JUNE 14

The great majority of Christians can recall some
incident in which their lives, in times of critical danger,
have been miraculously preserved—an almost plane crash,
a near car wreck, a fierce temptation. Though they
may have seen no angels, their presence could
explain why tragedy was averted.

JULY 20

The appearance of angels is awe-inspiring, something about them awakening fear in the human heart. They represent a presence that has greatness and sends a chill down the spine.

JUNE 13

$\mathcal{L}$ucifer was not satisfied with being subordinated to his creator. He wanted to usurp God's throne. He exulted at the thought of being the center of power throughout the universe—he wanted to be the Caesar, the Napoleon, the Hitler of the entire universe.

JULY 21

Angels, whether noticed by men or not, are active in our twentieth-century world. Are we aware of them?

JUNE 12

The Scriptures are full of dramatic evidences of the protective care of angels in their earthly service to the people of God.

Suddenly an angel of the Lord appeared and a light shone in the cell. He struck Peter on the side and woke him up. "Quick, get up!" he said, and the chains fell off Peter's wrist.

ACTS 12:7 NIV

JULY 22

In Daniel 6:22, we read, "My God hath sent his angel, and hath shut the lions' mouths." In the den, Daniel's sight evidently perceived the angelic presence, and the lions' strength more than met its match in the power of the angel.

JUNE 11

Thank God for the angelic forces that fight off the works of darkness. Angels never minister selfishly; they serve so that all glory may be given to God as believers are strengthened.

JULY 23

$\mathcal{W}$e are to rely on the Holy Spirit, who dwells within us and is willing and able to help us in every situation if we will turn to Him. In addition we can count on the powerful presence of angels.

JUNE 10

*M*any experiences in both Old and New Testaments grew out of the imprisonment of God's saints, calling either for God to deliver directly, or to intervene through angels acting in His name.

JULY 24

Angels cannot preach the gospel...rather, God has commanded the church to preach. This great task is reserved to believers. God has no other means. Only man can speak salvation's experience to man. God has, however, assigned angels to assist those who preach. Their assistance includes the use of miraculous and corroborating signs.

JUNE 9

*M*any today who are captive in the chains of depression can take courage to believe in the prospect of deliverance. God has no favorites and declares that angels will minister to all the heirs of faith.

JULY 25

While God has delegated angels to make special pronouncements for Him, He has not given them the privilege of proclaiming the gospel message.... Perhaps spirit-beings who have never experienced the effects of separation from fellowship with God because of sin would be unable to preach with understanding.

JUNE 8

In a loud voice they sang: "Worthy is the Lamb, who was slain, to receive power and wealth and wisdom and strength and honor and glory and praise!"

REVELATION 5:12 NIV

JULY 26

We often get false notions about angels from plays given by Sunday school children at Christmas. It is true that angels are ministering spirits sent to help the heirs of salvation. But just as they fulfill God's will in salvation for believers in Jesus Christ, so they are also "avengers" who use their great power to fulfill God's will in judgment.

JUNE 7

$\mathcal{A}$s to their number, David recorded twenty thousand coursing through the skyways of the stars. Even with his limited vision he impressively notes, "The chariots of God are twenty thousand, even thousands of angels (Psalm 68:17).

JULY 27

Unknown to men, angels have undoubtedly in the past helped destroy evil systems like Nazism, because those governments came to the place where God could no longer withhold His hand. These same angels will carry out fearful judgments in the future, some of which the Book of Revelation vividly describes.

JUNE 6

*W*hether or not we sense and feel the presence of the Holy Spirit or one of the holy angels, by faith we are certain God will never leave us nor forsake us.

JULY 28

We should always be grateful for the goodness of God, who uses these wonderful friends called angels to protect us. Evidence from Scripture as well as personal experience confirms to us that individual guardians, guiding angels, attend at least some of our ways and hover protectively over our lives.

JUNE 5

The writer of Hebrews speaks of angelic forces as executors of God's judgments: "Who maketh his angels spirits, and his ministers a flame of fire" (Hebrews 1:7). The flaming fire suggests how awful are the judgments of God and how burning is the power of the angels who carry out God's decisions. Angels administer judgment in accord with God's principles of righteousness.

JULY 29

Paul speaks the truth when he says that the forts of darkness are impregnable. Yet they yield to the warfare of faith and light as angel hosts press the warfare to gain the victory for us.

The weapons we fight with are not the weapons of the world. On the contrary, they have divine power to demolish strongholds.

2 CORINTHIANS 10:4 NIV

JUNE 4

We can describe all unrighteousness and transgression against God as "self-will" against the will of God. This definition applies to human beings today as well as to angels.

JULY 30

God uses both men and angels to declare His message to those who have been saved by grace. "Are they not all ministering spirits, sent forth to minister for them who shall be heirs of salvation?" (Hebrews 1:14).

JUNE 3

𝓛ucifer, the son of the morning, was created, as were all angels, for the purpose of glorifying God. However, instead of serving God and praising Him forever, Satan desired to rule over heaven and creation in the place of God. He wanted supreme authority!

JULY 31

𝒥ust as Jesus is with us now through the Holy Spirit, revealing himself and His will, so was He with His people in ages past, and so shall He be for all time to come, the angel of God's presence who leads us.

JUNE 2

*I*ntrinsically, angels do not possess physical bodies, although they may take on physical bodies when God appoints them to special tasks. Furthermore, God has given them no ability to reproduce, and they neither marry nor are given in marriage.

For when the dead rise, they will neither marry nor be given in marriage; they will be like the angels in heaven.

MARK 12:25 NIV

AUGUST 1

𝒜ngels minister to us personally. Many accounts in Scripture confirm that we are the subjects of their individual concern. In his book, *Table Talk*, Martin Luther said, "An angel is a spiritual creature created by God without a body, for the service of Christendom and the church."

JUNE 1

𝒮cripture dramatically underscores God's use of angels to execute His judgments. King Hezekiah had received a letter from the commander of the Assyrian forces and immediately sought God's counsel. God gave Isaiah the answer, saying that not one Assyrian arrow would be fired into the city. He promised to defend Jerusalem on that occasion for David's sake. Dramatically, that night, just one angel struck the Assyrian encampment and 185,000 soldiers were found dead on the field of battle the next morning.

AUGUST 2

No discordant note sounds among the angels of heaven. They are committed to fulfill the purpose for which all true children of God pray, "Thy kingdom come. Thy will be done...as it is in heaven" (Matthew 6:10).

MAY 31

*N*ew Testament history also records incidents where avenging angels judged the unrighteous acts of men and nations.... How fearful it is to have these mighty angels carry out the judgments of an all-powerful God.

AUGUST 3

Satan, who had fallen before he tempted Adam and Eve, was the agent and bears a greater guilt because there was no one to tempt him when he sinned; on the other hand, Adam and Eve were faced with a tempter.

MAY 30

Not angels, but the Holy Spirit convicts men of sin, righteousness, and judgment. He reveals and interprets Jesus Christ to men, while angels remain messengers of God who serve men as ministering spirits.

AUGUST 4

It is difficult to suppose that the fall of the angels before God placed Adam and Eve in the Garden. We know for a fact that God rested on the seventh day, or at the end of all creation, and pronounced everything to be good. By implication, up to this time even the angelic creation was good.

MAY 29

God has empowered angels to separate the sheep from the goats, the wheat from the chaff, and one of them will blow the trumpet that announces impending judgment when God summons the nations to stand before Him in the last great judgment.

AUGUST 5

The special angels of proclamation have faithfully
bridged the centuries, carrying the message of God's
will in times of oppression, discouragement,
and waning endurance.

MAY 28

The Christian should never consider death a tragedy. Rather he should see it as angels do: They realize that joy should mark the journey from time to eternity. The way to life is by the valley of death, but the road is marked with victory all the way.

AUGUST 6

As God's angels have watched the drama of this age unfolding, they have seen the Christian church established and expand around the world. They miss nothing as they watch the movements of time.

MAY 27

As the weeds are pulled up and burned in the fire, so it will be at the end of the age. The Son of Man will send out his angels, and they will weed out of his kingdom everything that causes sin and all who do evil.

MATTHEW 13:40,41 NIV

AUGUST 7

While the seraphim and the cherubim belong to different orders and are surrounded by much mystery in Scripture, they share one thing. They constantly glorify God.

Above him were seraphs.... And they were calling to one another: "Holy, holy, holy is the Lord Almighty; the whole earth is full of his glory."

ISAIAH 6:2,3 NIV

MAY 26

We are not called upon to obey the voice of angels. But we are to heed and obey the Word of God and the voice of God that calls upon us to be reconciled to Him by faith in Jesus Christ. If not, we will have to pay the penalty of unforgiven sin. The angels will administer that penalty.

AUGUST 8

𝒜ngels have their own reasons for singing, ones that differ from ours. They have given themselves to the service of God Almighty.... The cause they represent has been victorious; the fight they fought is finished.... The angels sing a different song. But they sing; my, how they sing!

MAY 25

*E*very son of Adam's race is confronted with two ways of life: one, to eternal life; the other, to eternal death. We have seen how angels execute God's judgment on those who reject Jesus; the angels cast them into the furnace of fire. But there is a totally different judgment: It is the good and wonderful judgment unto everlasting life.

AUGUST 9

The greatest catastrophe in the history of the universal creation was Lucifer's defiance of God and the consequent fall of perhaps one-third of the angels who joined him in his wickedness. When did it happen? Sometime between the dawn of creation and the intrusion of Satan into the Garden of Eden.

MAY 24

God's glory will not be denied, and every heavenly being gives silent or vocal testimony to the splendor of God.

Each of the four living creatures had six wings and was covered with eyes all around.... Day and night they never stop saying: "Holy, holy, holy is the Lord God Almighty, who was, and is, and is to come."

REVELATION 4:8 NIV

AUGUST 10

$\mathcal{T}$he angels who fell, fell because they had sinned against God. In 2 Peter 2:4, the Scripture says, "God spared not the angels that sinned but cast them down to hell, and delivered them into chains of darkness, to be reserved unto judgment."

MAY 23

Even as the angels escorted Lazarus when he died, so we can assume that they escorted Stephen; and so they will escort us when by death we are summoned into the presence of Christ.

AUGUST 11

As glorious as the angelic and heavenly beings are, they become dim beside the inexpressible glory resident in our heavenly Lamb, the Lord of glory, to whom all powers in heaven and on earth bow in holy worship and breathless adoration.

MAY 22

When you know Christ you need not fear God's judgment, for He has fully and completely purchased your salvation. Don't delay your decision for Christ, but open your heart to Him and you too will know the joy of sharing in His fellowship throughout all eternity in heaven.

AUGUST 12

𝒞herubim will not refuse the humblest Christian access to the throne. They assure us that we can come boldly— because of Christ's work on the cross!... The inner sanctuary of God's throne is always open to those who have repented of sin and trusted Christ as Savior.

MAY 21

[The apostle Paul] says that in fighting the organized kingdom of satanic darkness, we struggle against "the world forces of this darkness...the spiritual forces of wickedness in the heavenly places" (Ephesians 6:12, NASB).

AUGUST 13

It boggles the mind to try to imagine the kind of earth this is going to be when God eliminates the devil and sin. Our minds are staggered at the thought of "Christ on the throne...." The urge in man's heart toward immorality will have vanished. In that day the great drive in man will be a thirst for righteousness.

MAY 20

Certainly we are up against a gigantic war machine. But we are encompassed by a heavenly host so powerful that we need not fear the warfare—the battle is the Lord's.

AUGUST 14

Many people ask, "How could this conflict [between the holy angels and the fallen angels] come about in God's perfect universe?" The apostle Paul calls it "the mystery of iniquity."

For the mystery of lawlessness is already at work; only he who now restrains will do so until he is taken out of the way.

2 THESSALONIANS 2:7 NASB

MAY 19

No angel can enjoy sonship in Jesus or be partaker of the divine nature or become a joint heir with Jesus in His kingdom. You and I are a unique and royal priesthood in the universe, and we have privileges that even angels cannot experience.

AUGUST 15

Satan may appear to be winning the war because sometimes he wins important battles, but the final outcome is certain. One day he will be defeated and stripped of his powers eternally. God will shatter the powers of darkness.

MAY 18

> The Son of Man is going to come in his Father's glory with his angels, and then he will reward each person according to what he has done.
>
> MATTHEW 16:27 NIV

AUGUST 16

I am sending an angel ahead of you to guard you along the way and to bring you to the place I have prepared.

EXODUS 23:20 NIV

MAY 17

*I*ncrease Mather wrote centuries ago in *Angelographia*, "Angels both good and bad have a greater influence on this world than men are generally aware of. We ought to admire the grace of God toward us sinful creatures in that He hath appointed His holy angels to guard us against the mischiefs of wicked spirits who are always intending our hurt, both to our bodies and to our souls."

AUGUST 17

Angels want you to turn toward heaven,
but they know that this is a decision that you
and you alone will have to make.

MAY 16

If your valley is full of foes, raise your sights to the hills and see the holy angels of God arrayed for battle on your behalf.

AUGUST 18

The one and only way you can be converted is to believe on the Lord Jesus Christ as your own personal Lord and Savior. You don't have to straighten out your life first....
You have tried all that and failed many times.
You can come "just as you are."

MAY 15

When Jesus returns, He will be accompanied by the hosts of heaven. The holy angels will be with Him! "When the Son of man shall come in his glory, and all the holy angels with him, then shall he sit upon the throne of his glory" (Matthew 25:31).

AUGUST 19

𝒮atan, or the devil, was once called "Lucifer, the son of the morning." Along with Michael, he may have been one of the two archangels, but he was cast form heaven with his rebel forces and continues to fight.

MAY 14

God is recording not only the words and actions but all the thoughts and intents of our hearts. Someday you and I will have to give an account, and at that time our final destiny will be to determined by whether we have received or rejected Jesus.

AUGUST 20

I believe that angels and those of us who have been redeemed will compete with each other for the endless ages of eternity to see who can best ascribe glory and praise to our wonderful God!

MAY 13

The Bible says that a time will come when the crooked places will be made straight.

I will go before you and will level the mountains. I will break down gates of bronze and cut through bars of iron.

ISAIAH 45:2 NIV

AUGUST 21

It is my prayer that God will use this book to bring comfort to the sick and the dying; to bring encouragement to those who are under the pressures of everyday living; to bring guidance to those who are frustrated by the events of our generation.

MAY 12

Justice demands that the books of life be balanced, but without a final judgment this would be impossible.... Reason alone should tell us that there must come a time when God will call upon the Hitlers and the Ide Amins of the world for an accounting. Otherwise there is no justice in the universe.

AUGUST 22

The ministry of the seraphim is to praise the name and character of God in heaven. Their ministry relates directly to God and His heavenly throne, because they are positioned above the throne—unlike the cherubim, who are beside it.

O Lord Almighty, God of Israel, enthroned between the cherubim, you alone are God over all the kingdoms of the earth.

ISAIAH 37:16 NIV

MAY 11

[*L*ucifer's] "I will" spirit is the spirit of rebellion. His was a bold act to dethrone the Lord Most High. Here was a wicked schemer who saw himself occupying the superlative position of power and glory. He wanted to be worshiped, not to worship.

AUGUST 23

Scripture designates only Michael as an archangel.... The prefix "arch" suggests a chief, principal, or great angel. Thus, Michael is now the angel above all angels, recognized in rank to be the first prince of heaven. He is, as it were, the Prime Minister in God's administration of the universe, and is the "angel administrator" of God for judgment.

MAY 10

Satan's desire to replace God as ruler of the universe may have been rooted in a basic sin that leads to the sin of pride I have already mentioned. Underneath Satan's pride lurked the deadliest of all sins, the sin of covetousness. He wanted what did not belong to him.

AUGUST 24

We cannot study the subject of angels in the Bible without becoming aware of ranks among angelic beings. The evidence shows that they are organized in terms of authority and glory.

MAY 9

Our valleys may be filled with foes and tears; but we can lift our eyes to the hills to see God and the angels, heaven's spectators, who support us according to God's infinite wisdom as they prepare our welcome home.

AUGUST 25

In all their distress he too was distressed,
and the angel of his presence saved them. In his love
and mercy he redeemed them; he lifted them up
and carried them all the days of old.

ISAIAH 63:9 NIV

MAY 8

$\mathcal{T}$he Bible says we may see the angels God has sent, but fail to recognize them: "Be not forgetful to entertain strangers: for thereby some have entertained angels unawares" (Hebrews 13:2).

AUGUST 26

$\mathcal{T}$hink of it! Multitudes of angels, indescribably mighty, performing the commands of heaven! More amazingly, even one angel is indescribably mighty, as though an extension of the arm of God.

MAY 7

The angels of heaven have their eyes on every person. They know the spiritual condition of everybody on the face of the earth. Not only does God love you, but the angels love you too. They are anxious for you to repent and turn to Christ for salvation before it is too late.

AUGUST 27

𝒥ewish scholars called the angel of the Lord by the
name, "Metatron, the angel of countenance," because
He witnesses the countenance of God continuously
and, therefore, works to extend the program
of God for each of us.

MAY 6

Satan, the fallen prince of heaven, has made his decision to battle against God to the death.... In his warfare against God, Satan uses the human race, which God created and loved.

The Lord himself goes before you and will be with you; he will never leave you nor forsake you. Do not be afraid; do not be discouraged.

DEUTERONOMY 31:8 NIV

AUGUST 28

𝒜ngels revel in the power of the resurrection of Jesus, which assures us of our resurrection and guarantees us a safe passage to heaven.

MAY 5

Virtually every war ever fought began because of covetousness. The warfare in heaven and on earth between God and the devil certainly sprang from the same desire—the lust for what belonged to God alone.

AUGUST 29

While the sting of death has been removed by the work of Christ on the cross, and by His resurrection, yet the crossing of this valley still stimulates fear and mystery. However, angels will be there to help us. Could not the "rod and staff," which help us in the valley of the shadow of death (Psalm 23:4), be these holy angels?

MAY 4

It must give the angels great satisfaction to watch the Church of Jesus Christ minister the unsearchable riches of Christ to lost men everywhere.

There is rejoicing in the presence of the angels of God over one sinner who repents.

LUKE 15:10 NIV

AUGUST 30

Just as an angel was involved in Christ's resurrection, so will angels help us in death. Only one thin veil separates our natural world from the spiritual world. That thin veil we call death. However, Christ both vanquished death and overcame the dark threats of the evil fallen angels. So now God surrounds death with the assurance of angelic help to bring pulsing life out of the darkness of that experience for believers. We inherit the kingdom of God.

MAY 3

$\mathcal{Y}$ou can come to Christ right now wherever you are and just as your are—and the angels of heaven will rejoice!

AUGUST 31

[Satan and his angels] constitute a mighty force—
capable of wreaking havoc among individuals, families
and nations! Watch out, they are dangerous, vicious
and deadly. They want you under their control,
and they will pay any price to get you!

*Nothing will ever be able to separate
us from the love of God.*

ROMANS 8:39 TLB

MAY 2

As I look back over my life I remember the moment I came to Jesus Christ as Savior and Lord. The angels rejoiced! Since then I have been in thousands of battles with Satan and his demons. As I yielded my will and committed myself totally to Christ—as I prayed and believed—I am convinced that God "put a hedge about me," a hedge of angels to protect me.

SEPTEMBER 1

It is likely that John saw a massive heavenly choir (Revelation 5:11,12) of many millions who expressed their praise of the heavenly Lamb through magnificent music. I believe angel choirs will sing in eternity to the glory of God and the supreme delight of the redeemed.

MAY 1

The Scripture says there is a time to be born and a time to die. And when my time to die comes an angel will be there to comfort me. He will give me peace and joy even at that most critical hour, and usher me into the presence of God, and I will dwell with the Lord forever. Thank God for the ministry of His blessed angels!

SEPTEMBER 2

Angels possess the ultimate capacity to offer praise, and their music from time immemorial has been the primary vehicle of praise to our all-glorious God. Music is the universal language.

Praise the Lord from the heavens, praise him in the heights above. Praise him, all his angels, praise him, all his heavenly hosts.

PSALM 148:1,2 NIV

APRIL 30

Jesus Christ...has gone into heaven and is at God's right hand—with angels, authorities and powers in submission to him.

1 PETER 3:22 NIV

SEPTEMBER 3

In Psalm 103:20 David speaks about [God's] "angels that excel in strength." Nowhere in Scripture is that strength manifested more dramatically than in the climax of this age.... The Bible says that one angel will come from heaven. He will have a great chain in his hand. And then he will cast [Satan] into the pit. How great is the power of one of God's mighty angels.

APRIL 29

Although angels are glorious beings, the Scriptures make it clear that they differ from regenerated men in significant ways. How can angels understand how precious Jesus is to those for whom His death on Calvary brings light, life, and immortality?

SEPTEMBER 4

[God] gave a command to the skies above
and opened the doors of the heavens.... Men
ate the bread of angels; he sent them all
the food they could eat.

PSALM 78:23,25 NIV

APRIL 28

Satan is indeed capable of doing supernatural things—
but he can act only by the permissive will of God; he
is on a leash. It is God who is all-powerful. It is God
who is omnipotent. God has provided Christians
with both offensive and defensive weapons.

SEPTEMBER 5

*A*ngels probably know things about us that we do not know about ourselves. And because they are ministering spirits, they will always use this knowledge for our good and not for evil purposes.

APRIL 27

$\mathcal{G}$od commands angels to help men since they will be made higher than the angels at the resurrection.... God will alter the temporary lower position of man when the kingdom of God has come in its fullness.

Those who are considered worthy of taking part in that age and in the resurrection...can no longer die.... They are God's children, since they are children of the resurrection.

LUKE 20:35,36 NIV

SEPTEMBER 6

Angels possess knowledge that men do not have. But however vast is their knowledge, we can be sure they are not omniscient. They do not know everything. They are not like God. Jesus bore testimony to the limited knowledge of the angels when He was speaking of His Second Coming. In Mark 13:32, He said, "But of that day and that hour knoweth no man, no, not the angels which are in heaven."

APRIL 26

What fact could provide a greater motivation to righteous living than that? I must say to myself, "Careful, angels are watching!"

SEPTEMBER 7

Just as angels differ from people with respect to marriage, so they differ in other important ways. Nothing in Scripture says that angels must eat to stay alive. But the Bible says that on certain occasions angels in human form did indeed eat.

APRIL 25

Where the Lord works, Satan's forces hinder; where angel beings carry out their divine directives, the devils rage. All this comes about because the powers of darkness press their counterattack to recapture the ground held for the glory of God.

SEPTEMBER 8

When a person accepts God's gift of eternal life through Jesus Christ, angels set all the bells of heaven to ringing with their rejoicing before the Lamb of God.

APRIL 24

Although Satan and his evil followers press their warfare in the heavens, it seems that their primary endeavor is to destroy faith in the world. Isaiah 13:12-14 clearly points up Satan's objectives: he works to bring about the downfall of nations, to corrupt moral standards and to waste human resources.

SEPTEMBER 9

The Lord answered Job out of the storm. "Where were you when I laid the earth's foundations? Tell me, if you understand.... On what were its footings set, or who laid its cornerstone—while the morning stars sang together and all the angels shouted for joy?"

JOB 38:1,4,6,7 NIV

APRIL 23

Don't be afraid. God is for you. He has committed His angels to wage war in this conflict of the ages—and they will win the victory.

SEPTEMBER 10

The holy angels, who are ministering spirits, have never lost their original glory and spiritual relationship with God. This assures them of their exalted place in the royal order of God's creation.

APRIL 22

I am with you, and I will protect you
wherever you go.

GENESIS 28:15 TLB

SEPTEMBER 11

Although angels are glorious beings, the Scriptures make it clear that they differ from regenerated men in significant ways. Is it not strange that angels themselves will be judged by believers who were once sinners? Such judgment, however, apparently applies only to those fallen angels who followed Lucifer.

APRIL 21

The Bible indicates angels are more often invisible to human eyes. Whether visible or invisible, however, God causes His angels to go before us, to be with us, and to follow after us.

SEPTEMBER 12

Who can comprehend the overwhelming thrill of fellowship with God and the joy of salvation that even angels do not know?... The angels are aware of that joy.

There is rejoicing in the presence of the angels of God over one sinner who repents.

LUKE 15:10 NIV

APRIL 20

Angelic presences are in control of the battlefield about us, so that we may stand with complete confidence in the midst of the fight. "If God be for us who can be against us?" (Romans 8:31).

SEPTEMBER 13

Some angels remained behind [when Jesus ascended to heaven] to assure those early disciples that they would always be near, ready to help God's people throughout the ages to come—until Christ returns in person with the angelic hosts.

APRIL 19

Apparently angels have a beauty and variety that surpass anything known to men. Scripture does not tell us what elements make up angels. Nor can modern science, which is only beginning to explore the realm of the unseen, tell us about the constitution or even the work of angels.

SEPTEMBER 14

The angels escorted the resurrected Lord of glory back to be seated at the Father's right hand; then even the morning stars ascribed honor, glory, and praise to Him as the Son of the Living God.

APRIL 18

*G*od is forever imaginative, colorful, and glorious in what He designs. Some of the descriptions of angels, including the one of Lucifer in Ezekiel 28, indicate that they are exotic to the human eye and mind.

You were the model of perfection.... Every precious stone adorned you: ruby, topaz and emerald, chrysolite, onyx and jasper, sapphire, turquoise and beryl. Your settings and mountings were made of gold.

EZEKIEL 28:12,13 NIV

SEPTEMBER 15

Acts 1:9 says, "And when he had spoken these things, while they beheld, he was taken up; and a cloud received him out of their sight." Jesus had been accompanied to earth by an angelic host. I believe that the word "cloud" suggests that angels had come to escort Him back to the right hand of God the Father.

APRIL 17

The Bible seems to indicate that angels do not age, and never says that one was sick. Except for those who fell with Lucifer, the ravages of sin that have brought destruction, sickness, and chaos to our earth have not affected them. The holy angels will never die.

SEPTEMBER 16

*M*ary stood outside the tomb crying. As she wept, she bent over to look into the tomb and saw two angels in white, seated where Jesus' body had been, one at the head and the other at the foot.

JOHN 20:11,12 NIV

APRIL 16

The Bible teaches that angels are sexless. Jesus said that in heaven men "neither marry, nor are given in marriage, but are as the angels of God in heaven" (Matthew 22:30).

SEPTEMBER 17

One of the angels who was sitting outside the tomb proclaimed the greatest message the world has ever heard: "He is not here, but is risen" (Luke 24:6). Those few words changed the history of the universe. Darkness and despair died; hope and anticipation were born in the hearts of men.

APRIL 15

In some cases in the Old Testament God himself appeared in human form as an angel. This reinforces the idea of the relationship between God and His angels. Nevertheless, in almost all of the cases where angelic personages appear, they are God's created angelic beings and not God himself.

SEPTEMBER 18

No words of men or angels can adequately describe the height and depth, the length and breadth of the glory to which the world awakened when Jesus came forth to life from the pall of death.

APRIL 14

$\mathcal{S}$atan never yields an inch, nor does he ever pause in his opposition to the plan of God to redeem the "cosmos" from his control. He forever tries to discredit the truthfulness of the Word of God; he coaxes men to deny the authority of God; and he persuades the world to wallow in the deluding comforts of sin.

SEPTEMBER 19

The angels who came to the garden where Jesus' body lay rolled away the stone and permitted fresh air and morning light to fill His tomb. The sepulcher was no longer an empty vault or dreary dormitory; rather it was a life-affirming place that radiated the glory of the living God. No longer was it a dark prison but a transformed reminder of the celestial light that sweeps aside the shadows of death. Jesus' resurrection changed it.

APRIL 13

𝒢od assures us that through the work of Christ and the labors of His angelic deputies we can look for the triumphant and victorious warfare over the armies of Lucifer.

SEPTEMBER 20

I have often wondered what those guards
must have thought when, against the brightness
of the rising sun, they saw the angel rolling away the
gigantic boulder with possibly the lightest touch of
his finger! The guards, though heavily armed,
were paralyzed with fear.

APRIL 12

Angels have an important role in future events! Human history began at Eden where God planted a garden and made man for His eternal fellowship. Angels were there. They have never failed to attend to the human scene. And they will continue on the scene throughout the succeeding ages, till time runs into eternity.

SEPTEMBER 21

The keepers of the tomb shook and became as dead men [when they saw the angel who rolled away the stone from the tomb of Jesus]. Incidentally, that stone weighed several times more than a single man could move, yet the physical power of the angel was not taxed in rolling it aside.

APRIL 11

He will send his angels with a loud trumpet call, and they will gather his elect from the four winds, from one end of the heavens to the other.

MATTHEW 24:31 NIV

SEPTEMBER 22

Who can measure the brilliance of the lightning flash that illuminates the countryside for miles around? The angel who rolled away the stone from the tomb of Jesus was not only dressed in white, but shone as a flash of lightning with dazzling brilliance.

APRIL 10

Just as millions of angels participated in the dazzling
show when the morning stars sang together at creation,
so will the innumerable hosts of heaven help bring
to pass God's prophetic declarations throughout
time and into eternity.

SEPTEMBER 23

On the third day after [Jesus'] death the Bible says, "And behold there was a great earthquake; for the angel of the Lord descended from heaven, and came and rolled back the stone from the door, and sat upon it. His countenance was like lightning, and his raiment white as snow: And for fear of him the keepers did shake, and became as dead men" (Matthew 28:2-4).

APRIL 9

When God decrees it, Satan (Lucifer) will
be removed from the world of disorder so God can
establish righteousness everywhere, and a true theocracy.
Not until that event takes place will the human race
know perfect peace on earth.

SEPTEMBER 24

A light was kindled that day at Calvary. The cross blazed with the glory of God as the most terrible darkness was shattered by the light of salvation.

APRIL 8

God will use the angels to merge time into eternity, creating a new kind of life for every creature. Even today's intellectual world speaks of a point when time will be no more. Most scientists agree that the clock of time is running out.... Will man destroy himself? No!
God has another plan!

At the time they will see the Son of Man coming in a cloud with power and great glory.

LUKE 21:27 NIV

SEPTEMBER 25

Sin cost God His very best. Is it any wonder that the angels veiled their faces, that they were silent in their consternation as they witnessed the outworking of God's plan? How inconceivable it must have seemed to them, when they considered the fearful depravity of sin, that Jesus should shoulder it all. But they were soon to unveil their faces and offer their praises again.

APRIL 7

Christ is coming in great power, and all His holy angels will be with Him.... Angels figure prominently in the prophetic plan of God that continues on into the future events of Bible prophecy.

SEPTEMBER 26

No sin has been committed in the world today that can compare with the full cup of the universe's sin that brought Jesus to the cross. The question hurled toward heaven throughout the ages has been, "Who is He and why does He die?" The answer comes back, "This is My only begotten Son, dying not only for your sins but for the sins of the whole world."

APRIL 6

$\mathcal{E}$ach period of history seemingly has its own trials and convulsions. Each generation seems to have to "fight it out." Behind it all is the unseen struggle of the ages.... Light shines at the end of the tunnel.... The Bible declares that righteousness will eventually triumph, Utopia will come to earth, the kingdom of God will ultimately prevail. In bringing all this about angels will have a prominent part.

SEPTEMBER 27

We can never plumb the depths of sin, or sense how terrible human sin is, until we go to the cross and see that it was "sin" that caused the Son of God to be crucified.... To you sin may be a small thing; to God it is a great and awful thing. It is the second largest thing in the world; only the love of God is greater.

APRIL 5

The prophets spoke of a wonderful day when God would lift the curse, when lion and lamb would lie down together, and when nations would learn war no more (Isaiah 2:4; 11:6). Angel hosts will fulfill His royal decrees and oversee God's purpose in the universe.

SEPTEMBER 28

The angels were under orders not to intervene at this terrible, holy moment. Even the angels could not minister to the Son of God at Calvary. He died alone to take the full death penalty you and I deserved.

APRIL 4

It will be a victorious day for the universe, and especially planet earth, when the devil and his angels are thrown into the lake of fire, never again to tempt and destroy man. To the angels God has assigned this task, and Scripture assures us that they will be victorious.

SEPTEMBER 29

The angels would have come to the cross to rescue
the King of kings, but because of His love for the
human race and because He knew it was only
through His death that they could be saved,
He refused to call for their help.

APRIL 3

The Son of Man will send out his angels, and they will weed out of his kingdom everything that causes sin and all who do evil. They will throw them into the fiery furnace, where there will be weeping and gnashing of teeth. Then the righteous will shine like the sun in the kingdom of their Father. He who has ears, let him hear.

MATTHEW 13:41-43 NIV

SEPTEMBER 30

The tragedy of sin reached its crescendo when God in Christ became sin.... He knew He could come down [from the cross] if He chose; He knew He could get help from more than twelve legions of angels who hovered about with drawn swords. Yet for our salvation He stayed there.

APRIL 2

We who have made our peace with God should be like the evangelist D. L. Moody. When he was aware that death was at hand, he said, "Earth recedes, heaven opens before me." It appeared as though he was dreaming. Then he said, "No, this is no dream...it is beautiful, it is like a trance. If this is death, it is sweet. There is no valley here. God is calling me, and I must go."

OCTOBER 1

The night before His crucifixion Jesus was in the
Garden of Gethsemane.... The Son of man was all alone.
He prayed, "Father, if thou be willing, remove this cup
from me: nevertheless not my will, but thine, be done"
(Luke 22:42). Then it was at that crucial moment that
the angel came to assist Him, "strengthening Him."
The Greek work for strengthening is *eniskuo*,
which means to make strong inwardly.

APRIL 1

Angelic ambassadors supported, strengthened, and sustained [Jesus after His temptation in the wilderness]. From that moment on our Lord Jesus Christ, "who has been tempted in every way, just as we are—yet was without sin" (Hebrews 4:15, NIV), could sympathize and help Christian believers for the ages to come, and lead them to victory in their hour of temptation.

OCTOBER 2

$\mathcal{L}$et us believe that angels are here among us. They may not laugh or cry with us, but we do know they delight with us over every victory in our evangelistic endeavors. Jesus taught that "there is joy in the presence of the angels of God when one sinner repents" (Luke 15:10, TLB).

MARCH 31

We are not alone in this world! The Bible teaches us that God's Holy Spirit has been given to empower us and guide us. In addition, the Bible—in nearly three hundred different places—also teaches that God has countless angels at His command.

OCTOBER 3

The ministering angels will see us safely across the Jordan River of death as we enter the promised land of heaven. So the Christian does not sorrow as those who have no hope.

We are saved by trusting. And trusting means looking forward to getting something we don't yet have.

ROMANS 8:24 TLB

MARCH 30

The empire of angels is as vast as God's creation. If you believe the Bible, you will believe in their ministry. They crisscross the Old and New Testaments, being mentioned directly or indirectly nearly three hundred times.

OCTOBER 4

God uses angels to work out the destinies of men and nations. He has altered the courses of the busy political and social arenas of our society and directed the destinies of men by angelic visitation many times over.

MARCH 29

Both Daniel and John described the glories of the angels...visible descending from heaven with immeasurable beauty and brilliance, shining like the sun.

Then I saw another mighty angel coming down from heaven. He was robed in a cloud, with a rainbow above his head; his face was like the sun, and his legs were like fiery pillars.

REVELATION 10:1 NIV

OCTOBER 5

While all men are sinners by nature, choice, and practice, yet it is their deliberate rejection of Jesus Christ as Savior and Lord that causes the judgment of eternal separation from God.

The wages of sin is death, but the free gift of God is eternal life through Jesus Christ our Lord.

ROMANS 6:23 TLB

MARCH 28

*O*ught not Christians, grasping the eternal dimension of life, become conscious of the sinless angelic powers who are for real, and who associate with God himself and administer His works in our behalf?

OCTOBER 6

When God brings his firstborn into the world, he says, "Let all God's angels worship him." In speaking of the angels he says, "He makes his angels winds, his servants flames of fire."

HEBREWS 1:6,7 NIV

MARCH 27

You may be filled with dread at the thought of death. Just remember that at one moment you may be suffering, but in another moment, you will be instantly transformed into the glorious likeness of our Savior. The wonders, beauties, splendor, and grandeur of heaven will be yours. You will be surrounded by these heavenly messengers sent by God to bring you home.

OCTOBER 7

In dying [Christ] was forsaken by men, by angels, and by the Father who is of purer eyes than to look upon sin and who in His Son's atoning agony turned His face from Him. That is why Jesus cried from the cross, "My God, my God, why hast thou forsaken me?" (Matthew 27:46). He died alone. Angels were ready to rescue Him, but He refused.

MARCH 26

This is how it will be at the end of the age. The angels will come and separate the wicked from the righteous.

MATTHEW 13:49 NIV

OCTOBER 8

*N*either man nor angel could ever understand what was implied in the "cup" Jesus took in the Garden of Gethsemane that was to lead to His awful suffering, condemnation, and death.... The angels would have helped Him in that hour, but Christ did not call for their help. This one who said "No" to angel help said, in effect, "I will die for the sins of men because I love them so much."

MARCH 25

Angels enjoy far greater power than men, but they are not omnipotent or "all powerful." In 2 Thessalonians 1:7, Paul refers to the "mighty angels of God." From the word translated "mighty" here we get the English word dynamite. In material power, angels are God's dynamite!

OCTOBER 9

Angels are mightier than men, but they are not gods and they do not possess the attributes of the Godhead.

MARCH 24

In all these manifestations of angels we see God willing that men should know of His glory. He determines to maintain an adequate witness to that glory in both terrestrial and celestial realms.

OCTOBER 10

We should not confuse angels, whether visible or invisible, with the Holy Spirit, the third person of the Trinity and himself God. Angels do not indwell men; the Holy Spirit seals them and indwells them when He has regenerated them.

MARCH 23

We can be sure that there is no contradiction or competition between God the Holy Spirit and God's command of the angelic hosts. God himself is in control to accomplish His will—and in that we can rejoice!

OCTOBER 11

They went to the tomb early this morning but didn't find his body. They came and told us that they had seen a vision of angels, who said he was alive.

LUKE 24:22,23 NIV

MARCH 22

It is clear in Scripture that angels will be God's emissaries to carry out His judgment against those who deliberately reject Jesus Christ and the salvation God offers through Him.

OCTOBER 12

It's no less than heretical, and indeed is a breach of the first commandment, to worship any manifestations....only the Triune God is to be the object of our worship and of our prayers.

MARCH 21

Gabriel told Daniel that sin is a reality and must be paid for. The Messiah will do this by being cut off; that is, He will die for the sins of men. Then the power of sin to separate us from God will end and men will be reconciled to Him.

To put an end to sin to atone for wickedness, to bring in everlasting righteousness.

DANIEL 9:24 NIV

OCTOBER 13

It is no mere accident that angels are usually invisible. Though God in His infinite wisdom does not, as a rule, permit angels to take on physical dimensions, people tend to venerate them in a fashion that borders on worship. We are warned against worshiping the creature rather than the Creator.

They exchanged the truth of God for a lie, and worshiped and served created things rather than the Creator— who is forever praised. Amen.
ROMANS 1:25 NIV

MARCH 20

One of Satan's sly devices is to divert our minds from the help God offers us in our struggles against the forces of evil. However, the Bible testifies that God has provided assistance for us in our spiritual conflicts.

OCTOBER 14

Have you ever seen a pure spirit? I can't say that I have. Yet I do know that down through the ages God has chosen to manifest His own spiritual presence in different ways.... God has chosen also to manifest His presence through His angels, who are lesser beings to whom He has given the power to assume forms that occasionally make them visible to men.

MARCH 19

Angels have ministered the message, "All is well," to satisfy fully the physical, material, emotional, and spiritual needs of His people. They could testify, "The angel of the Lord came unto me."

OCTOBER 15

The Bible teaches about angels as oracles of God
who give divine or authoritative decisions and
bring messages from God to men. To fulfill this
function angels have not infrequently
assumed visible, human form.

MARCH 18

Jesus Christ the incarnate God, the second person of the Trinity, who is Creator of all things and by whom all things exist, is worthy of our worship; we are not to pray to angels.

OCTOBER 16

Believers, look up—take courage. The angels are nearer than you think. For after all...God has given "his angels charge of you, to guard you in all your ways. On their hands they will bear you up, lest you dash your foot against a stone" (Psalm 91:11,12, RSV).

MARCH 17

We see Jesus, who was made a little lower than the angels, now crowned with glory and honor because he suffered death, so that by the grace of God he might taste death for everyone.

HEBREWS 2:9 NIV

OCTOBER 17

The devil is alive and more at work than at any other time. The Bible says that since he realizes his time is short, his activity will increase. Through his demonic influences he does succeed in turning many away from true faith; but we can still say that his evil activities are countered for the people of God by His ministering spirits, the holy ones of the angelic order.

MARCH 16

I think before we can understand the music of heaven we will have to go beyond our earthly concept of music. I think most earthly music will seem to us to have been in the "minor key" in comparison to what we are going to hear in heaven.

OCTOBER 18

Perhaps the most difficult period in the life of Jesus before His crucifixion was His temptation by the devil in the wilderness.... Three times Satan attempted to defeat Jesus. Three times Jesus quoted Scripture, and three times Satan went down to defeat.... It was at this point that angels came to His assistance—not to help Him resist Satan as they help us, for He did that by himself, but to help Him after the battle was won.

MARCH 15

$\mathcal{G}$od gives the angels a place in this [wonderful judgment unto everlasting life] too. He commissions them to escort each believer to heaven and to give him a royal welcome as he enters the eternal presence of God. Each of us who trusts Christ will witness the rejoicing of angelic hosts around the throne of God.

OCTOBER 19

The Spirit sent [Jesus] out into the desert, and he was in the desert forty days, being tempted by Satan. He was with wild animals, and angels attended him.

MARK 1:12,13 NIV

MARCH 14

God has made men head over all the creatures of our earthly world; but they are lower than angels with respect to their bodies and to their place while here on earth.

OCTOBER 20

$\mathcal{T}$he holy ones of the angelic order are vigorous in delivering the heirs of salvation from the stratagems of evil men. They cannot fail.

MARCH 13

Whether the battle between the forces of Satan and the forces of God involve other planets and galaxies we do not know. But we do know that the earth is the scene of the conflict; however, it is a gigantic struggle that affects the entire universe.... It is almost incredible to us that supernatural beings from outer space are engaged in a struggle for this planet.

OCTOBER 21

Every true believer in Christ should be encouraged and strengthened! Angels are watching; they mark our path. They superintend the events of our lives and protect the interest of the Lord God, always working to promote His plans and to bring about His highest will for us.

MARCH 12

Someone has said, "When I die I do not want justice—I want mercy!" That mercy has been provided by the Lord Jesus Christ.

For all...are justified freely by his grace through the redemption that came by Jesus Christ.

ROMANS 3:23,24 NIV

OCTOBER 22

*I*n the New Testament John tells us of having seen ten thousand times ten thousand angels ministering to the Lamb of God in the throne room of the universe.

Then I looked and heard the voice of many angels, numbering thousands upon thousands, and ten thousand times ten thousand. They encircled the throne.

REVELATION 5:11 NIV

MARCH 11

Michael...is God's messenger of law and judgment. In this capacity he appears in Revelation 12:7-12 leading the armies that battle Satan, the great dragon, and all of his demons.... Scripture tells us in advance that Michael will finally be victorious in the battle. Hell will tremble; heaven will rejoice and celebrate!

OCTOBER 23

Reports continually flow to my attention from many places around the world telling of visitors of the angelic order appearing, ministering, fellowshiping and disappearing. They warn of God's impending judgment; they spell out the tenderness of His love; they meet a desperate need; then they are gone.

MARCH 10

There was war in heaven. Michael and his angels fought against the dragon, and the dragon and his angels fought back. But he was not strong enough, and they lost their place in heaven. The great dragon was hurled down—that ancient serpent, called the devil, or Satan, who leads the whole world astray. He was hurled to the earth, and his angels with him.

REVELATION 12:7-9 NIV

OCTOBER 24

Praise the Lord, you his angels, you mighty ones who do his bidding, who obey his word.

PSALM 103:20 NIV

MARCH 9

Although the angels rejoice when people are saved and glorify God who has saved them, they cannot do one thing: testify personally to something they have not experienced. They can only point to the experiences of the redeemed and rejoice that God has saved them.

OCTOBER 25

Angels speak. They appear and reappear. They are emotional creatures. While angels may become visible by choice, our eyes are not constructed to see them ordinarily any more than we can see the dimensions of a nuclear field, the structure of atoms, or the electricity that flows through copper wiring.

MARCH 8

While it is partly speculative, I believe that angels have the capacity to employ heavenly celestial music. Many dying believers have testified that they have heard the music of heaven.

OCTOBER 26

Daniel, while in prayer, records Gabriel's second appearance to him: "While I was speaking in prayer, the man Gabriel, whom I had seen in the former vision, being caused to fly swiftly, came near to me and touched me" (Daniel 9:21, AB).

MARCH 7

$\mathcal{A}$ngels...have had a part in bringing in the kingdom of God. They have helped the children of God in difficult circumstances. So theirs shall be a shout and a song of victory.

OCTOBER 27

Gabriel is one of the most prominent angels mentioned in Scripture. Gabriel, in Hebrew, means "God's hero," or "the mighty one," or "God is great." Scripture frequently refers to him as "the messenger of Jehovah" or "the Lord's messenger."

MARCH 6

The Bible guarantees every believer an escorted journey into the presence of Christ by the holy angels. The angelic emissaries of the Lord are often sent not only to catch away the redeemed of the Lord at death, but also to give hope and joy to those who remain, and to sustain them in their loss. He has promised to give "the oil of joy for mourning, the garment expressive of praise."

OCTOBER 28

Taking one of the stones there, [Jacob] put it under his head and lay down to sleep. He had a dream in which he saw a stairway resting on the earth, with its top reaching to heaven, and the angels of God were ascending and descending on it.

GENESIS 28:11,12 NIV

MARCH 5

If the activities of the devil and his demons seem to be intensifying in these days, as I believe they are, should not the incredibly greater supernatural powers of God's holy angels be even more indelibly impressed on the minds of people of faith?... Christians must never fail to sense the operation of angelic glory. It forever eclipses the world of demonic powers, as the sun does the candle's light.

OCTOBER 29

God placed angelic sentinels called cherubim at the east of the Garden of Eden. They were commissioned not only to bar man's return into Eden, but with "a flaming sword flashing back and forth to guard the way to the tree of life" (Genesis 3:24, NIV) lest Adam by eating of its fruit should live forever. If Adam had lived in his sin forever—this earth would long ago have been hell. Thus, in one sense, death is a blessing to the human race.

MARCH 4

We are not to be fearful; we are not to be distressed; we are not to be deceived; nor are we to be intimidated. Rather, we are to be on our guard, calm and alert, "Lest Satan should get an advantage of us: for we are not ignorant of his devices" (2 Corinthians 2:11).

OCTOBER 30

𝓕rom earliest antiquity, when the angel guardians of the gates to the glory of Eden sealed the entrance to the home of Adam and Eve, angels have manifested their presence in the world.

MARCH 3

I believe the time has come to focus on the positive of the Christian faith. John the Apostle said, "Greater is he that is in you, than he that is in the world" (1 John 4:4).

OCTOBER 31

$\mathcal{T}$he history of virtually all nations and cultures reveals at least some belief in angelic beings.... But no matter what the traditions, our frame of reference must be the Scripture as our supreme authority on this subject.

MARCH 2

It is my prayer that you would go forth in faith each day trusting God's constant watch-care over you.

NOVEMBER 1

*Singly or corporately, angels are for real.
They are better organized than were the armies of
Alexander the Great, Napoleon, or Eisenhower.*

MARCH 1

$\mathcal{G}$od's judgment will be so pure that even those who are condemned will bow their knee and confess, "Thou art just."

At the name of Jesus every knee should bow, in heaven and on earth and under the earth.

PHILIPPIANS 2:10 NIV

NOVEMBER 2

$\mathcal{P}$aul in 2 Thessalonians 1:7 says, "The Lord Jesus shall be revealed from heaven with his mighty angels."

FEBRUARY 29

Angels seemed to communicate terse commands. Often the angel messengers urged haste, and this is understandable since they were communicating a directive from God.... The angel said to Peter, "Rise quickly." The angel said to Gideon, "Arise and go in this thy might." The angel said to Joseph, "Go quickly," and to Philip, "Arise and go." In the same way any evangelistic ministry sounds the note of urgency concerning the gospel.

NOVEMBER 3

$\mathcal{T}$he Book of Revelation…says that armies of angels will appear with Jesus at the Battle of Armageddon when God's foes gather for their final defeat.

FEBRUARY 28

All the angels were standing around the throne and around the elders and the four living creatures. They fell down on their faces before the throne and worshiped God, saying: "Amen! Praise and glory and wisdom and thanks and honor and power and strength be to our God for ever and ever. Amen!"

REVELATION 7:11,12 NIV

NOVEMBER 4

Michael, the archangel, will shout as he accompanies Jesus at His Second Coming. Not only does he proclaim the matchless and exciting news that Jesus Christ returns, but he speaks the word of life to all who are dead in Christ and who await their resurrection.

For the Lord himself shall descend from heaven
with a shout, with the voice of the archangel...
and the dead in Christ shall rise first.

1 THESSALONIANS 4:16

FEBRUARY 27

Today we have the choice of whether or not to receive the ministry of angels. In choosing to follow Jesus Christ we also choose the protective watch and care of the angels of heaven. In the time of the Second Coming, we will no longer be afforded the privilege of choice. If we delay now, it will be too late, and we forfeit forever the gracious ministry of angels and the promise of salvation to eternal life.

NOVEMBER 5

Millions of angels are at God's command and at our service.... The hosts of heaven stand at attention as we make our way from earth to glory.

FEBRUARY 26

Dr. Miller asks the question, "What does the future hold for this weary old world?... The answers to such questions are not to be found in astrology or necromancy but in the divinely inspired Word of God. And we may be certain that, as the passing of time fulfills the prophetic Scriptures, the holy angels will be deeply involved in the fulfillment."

NOVEMBER 6

𝒫aul reminds us that there is a language of men and a language of angels (1 Corinthians 13:1). Angels have a celestial language and make music that is worthy of the God who made them. I believe in heaven we will be taught the language and music of the celestial world.

FEBRUARY 25

Many of us despair of coping with the pressures of our lives, but if we are living Spirit-filled and Spirit-directed lives, we can claim God's promises. The prophetic Scriptures give us "hope."

NOVEMBER 7

While we do not place our faith directly in angels,
we should place it in the God who rules the angels;
then we can have peace.

FEBRUARY 24